ARCTURUS

This edition published in 2017 by Arcturus Publishing Limited
26/27 Bickels Yard, 151–153 Bermondsey Street,
London SE1 3HA

Photography by Sally Henry, Trevor Cook and Shutterstock except for
p6-7 Javier Trueba/MSF/Science Photo Library; p42-43 Ocean/Corbis;
p62-63, p76-77, p102-103, p210-211, and p252-253 NASA;
p86-87 Wikipedia Commons; p112-113 Science Photo Library
(Steve Gschmeissner); and 142-143 Photo Researchers/FLPA.
3-D images on p90-91 by Pinsharp 3D Graphics
Illustrations by Andrew Painter
Design by Notion Design

ISBN: 978-1-78404-679-8
CH004567US

Supplier 29, Date 0717, Print run 6475

Printed in China

Introduction

This book is jam-packed full of supercool science experiments for you to amaze your family and friends with. Some of the experiments are really simple, while others are a little bit tricky and may need more equipment or the help of an adult.

Every experiment includes a list of all the equipment you'll need to do it. We've made sure all of these items are easy to get hold of, so you can get started with the fun part—doing the experiment.

We've also added a scientific explanation of each experiment in the panel "How does it work?" That way, you can astound your friends and family with your incredible scientific knowledge.

Have fun!

Contents

MATERIAL WORLD

Everything around you is made of matter. In fact, everything inside you is, too! In this chapter, you'll find facts and experiments that explore the incredible science of materials.

Thousands of years ago, water containing a mineral named gypsum filtered slowly through these caves, forming the enormous pillars you can see in this photograph.

Lava Lamp

Lava lamps are cool decorations that are fascinating to look at. They are also surprisingly simple to make.

You will need

- A clean plastic bottle or jar
- A funnel
- Vegetable oil
- Food coloring
- Effervescent vitamin tablet
- A flashlight
- Water

Step 1

Fill a bottle or jar ¼ full with water. Add 10 drops of food coloring.

Step 2

Fill the bottle to the top with vegetable oil.

Step 3

Break the vitamin tablet into four small pieces.

Step 4

Drop one piece of the vitamin tablet into the bottle. Watch the result!

Step 5

To improve the lava lamp effect, turn off the lights, turn on the flashlight, and shine it through the bottle.

Step 6

Experiment with different jars and bottles and other food colorings. Which work the best?

How does it work?

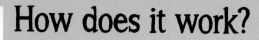

Oil and water do not mix. When you add oil to water, it usually just sits on its own in a separate layer on top of the water. However, adding the piece of tablet to the container changes this. The tablet reacts with the water, creating bubbles of carbon dioxide gas that rise to the surface. The oil and water are stirred up by the bubbles.

Mint Volcano

You will need

- Two packages of strawberry-flavored jello
- A pack of chewy mints
- Hot water
- A large mixing bowl
- A small glass
- A can of diet cola
- A plate
- A tray

Get ready for an edible eruption! In this experiment, you'll discover that mixing chewy mints and diet cola can have explosive results.

Step 1

Take two packages of jello. Follow the instructions on the package to make a jello mixture.

WARNING!
Ask an adult to help you with the hot water.

Step 2

Take a big bowl. Turn a glass upside down inside it.

Step 3

Pour the jello mixture into the bowl. Make sure it covers the glass.

Step 4

Put the jello in the refrigerator to set. When the jello has set, turn it out onto a flat plate and remove the glass.

Step 5

Put the plate onto a tray. Take the jello outside, then pour diet cola into the cavity left by the glass.

Step 6

Drop six chewy mints into the cola. Watch out—it will erupt!

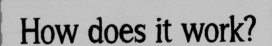

How does it work?

The bubbles in a cola drink are made up of carbon dioxide gas. They have been forced into the drink under pressure. When you drop a chewy mint into the cola, the carbon dioxide bubbles collect together and grow in the tiny dents on the surface of the mint. Then the bubbles rush out in a big eruption.

Balloon Kebab

If someone told you they could stick a sharp object through a balloon without popping it, you wouldn't believe them would you? But it is possible. Amaze your family and friends by making a genuine balloon kebab.

You will need

- Balloons
- A wooden kebab skewer
- Vegetable oil

Step 1

Blow up a balloon to about half its full size, and tie a knot in the neck.

Step 2

Hold the balloon in one hand and the kebab skewer in the other.

Step 3

Poke the point of the skewer into the balloon, near the knot. Wipe a little vegetable oil on the skewer, so that the skewer slides in smoothly.

Step 4

Push the skewer through the balloon very gently, twisting as you push. Aim to make it come out on the opposite side, at the middle of the top of the balloon.

Step 5

If you have a long skewer or small balloons, try to add more balloons—like a kebab!

If you poke the balloon in the middle with the skewer, it will pop!

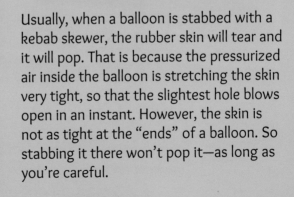

How does it work?

Usually, when a balloon is stabbed with a kebab skewer, the rubber skin will tear and it will pop. That is because the pressurized air inside the balloon is stretching the skin very tight, so that the slightest hole blows open in an instant. However, the skin is not as tight at the "ends" of a balloon. So stabbing it there won't pop it—as long as you're careful.

Magnetic Cereal

Is the iron contained in food the same thing as the metal iron? Try this experiment to find out.

You will need

- Cereal fortified with iron (look at the small print on the box)
- A rolling pin
- A small plastic bag
- A very strong magnet—a "rare earth" magnet will work well
- A cereal bowl
- Water

The bag keeps the cereal together.

Step 1

Crush some cereal into a fine powder in a small bag.

Step 2

Put the magnet in the powder and roll it around.

Try shaking the powder off—the magnetic attraction won't let you!

Step 3

Take the magnet out of the bag. It should have crumbs of cereal sticking to it.

Step 4

Take a clean cereal bowl and fill it almost to the top with water.

Step 5

When the water has stopped any movement, drop a large flake of cereal on the surface, in the middle of the bowl.

Step 6

By holding your magnet just above the cereal flake, you should be able to draw it across the surface of the water without touching it!

How does it work?

This experiment shows that fortified cereals, like many other foods, contain iron in small amounts. It is very important that you get enough iron in your diet. Iron helps your blood to carry oxygen around the body. If you don't have enough of it, you may feel tired and unwell.

Fossil Focus

When an animal or plant dies, it usually decays quickly. But sometimes an animal's body sinks into deep mud and lies there, undisturbed, for millions of years. As time passes, the mud presses down on the remains. Minerals dissolved in the mud turn the remains to stone. These remains are called fossils. Fossils give us clues about what life was like on Earth millions of years ago. Without fossils, we wouldn't know about dinosaurs or prehistoric sea creatures like this one.

Bubble Bomb

This fun and safe "bomb" will explode with a loud pop!

You will need

- Water
- A measuring cup
- A plastic ziplock bag
- A paper towel
- 2 tablespoons of baking soda
- Vinegar

Step 1

Find a place where making a mess won't be terrible—outside, or maybe in the bathtub if the weather's bad.

Step 2

Test your bag for leaks. Put water in it, close the seal, and turn it upside down. If no water leaks out, it's OK to use.

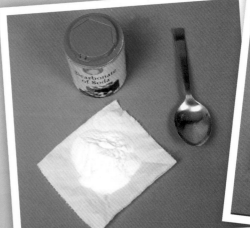

Step 3

Tear a piece of paper towel, about 5 inches (15 cm) square. Put 2 tablespoons of baking soda in the center of the square and fold the paper around it.

Step 4

Mix 10 fluid ounces (300 ml) of vinegar with 5 fluid ounces (150 ml) of warm water, then pour them into the plastic bag.

Step 5

Put the paper towel package into the bag. Hold it in the corner away from the vinegar while you seal the bag.

Step 6

Place the bag on the floor—and stand back! The bag will swell up ...

Step 7

... and then pop!

How does it work?

Vinegar is an acid and baking soda is a base. When you mix acids and bases together, they react and turn into different chemicals. When carbon dioxide gas forms in our experiment, there isn't enough room for it in the plastic bag. So the pressure builds up, and the bag swells and pops, releasing the gas.

Gloopy Goop

This strange slime is not really a liquid but not really a solid, either! Make some for yourself to find out what kind of material it is.

You will need

- 1 cup of cornflour
- ½ cup of water
- A mixing bowl
- Food coloring

Step 1

Pour a cup of cornflour into a mixing bowl. It should feel smooth and silky in your hands.

Step 2

Add two drops of food coloring to the water. You really don't need very much!

Step 3

Mix the water into the flour, using your fingers. How does the mixture feel now?

Step 4

Try squeezing a handful of the liquid you've made into a ball. It will become a solid!

Step 5

Let the goop settle into the bottom of the bowl. Touch the surface gently, then tap it hard.

Step 6

If you hold your hand still, it will become liquid and run through your fingers.

How does it work?

When this mixture is put under pressure, the cornflour molecules are forced together and it behaves like a solid. When it is handled gently, the cornflour molecules can move around freely, and it flows like a liquid. Quicksand works in just the same way!

Coin Cleaner

Many people like to collect coins from different countries. However, coins tarnish easily and can soon start to look dirty. Here is how you can give them back their shine.

You will need

- Dirty coins
- Cola
- A plastic cup
- A paper towel
- An old toothbrush

Step 1

Take some dirty coins. Why not take a photograph to compare results later on?

Step 2

Rinse a coin in water to remove any loose dirt.

Step 3

Put the coin in a plastic cup, then pour in some cola.

Step 4

After 20 minutes, take the coin out and dry it.

Step 5

Repeat the process until the coin is clean. With a really dirty coin, it may help to scrub the cola on the coin using an old toothbrush.

Step 6

Take photos of your coin at intervals to see the rate of change. Here's a very dirty old coin, with results after 30 minutes, 2 hours, 6 hours, 12 hours, and a day.

How does it work?

Cola drinks are more acidic than you might think! The cola wears down the top layer of the coins. That makes them look sparkly and clean.

Crystal Creations

A crystal is a solid material that forms itself into a very regular 3-D pattern. Crystals form when liquid cools, hardens, and turns into a solid. The arrangement of atoms in the solid produces the shape of the crystal. An example of this is when water is cooled and becomes ice.

Experiment 1

You will need

- Coarse string
- An ice pop stick
- Hot water
- A spoon
- Salt, sand, soil, sugar
- 2 glass jars
- A plastic bag
- Coffee filter paper or paper towel
- A funnel
- A small plate

Step 1

Put some hot water into a glass jar. Water from the hot faucet should be hot enough.

Step 2

Add sugar, one spoon at a time, using the ice pop stick to stir. Keep adding more sugar until you can't dissolve any more. You'll see undissolved sugar left at the bottom of the jar.

Step 3

Tie the string to the ice pop stick, hang it in the sugar solution, and leave to cool. The string is a good surface for growing crystals.

water level

end of string

Step 4

As the solution cools, crystals begin to form on the string. Be patient: It can take a few days for crystals to form, provided you have made a saturated solution.

How does it work?

The sugar dissolves in water to form a sugar solution. Hot water allows more sugar to dissolve. As the water cools, it cannot hold as much sugar in solution, and some sugar changes back to a solid.

Experiment 2

Step 1

Mix salt, soil, and sand together thoroughly with a spoon, on a piece of plastic bag.

Step 2

Stir the mixture into warm water. Leave it to settle overnight.

Step 3

Place the filter paper in a funnel, then pour the liquid through, being careful to leave the sediment in the bottom of the jar. Leave the filtered liquid on the plate in a warm place.

How does it work?

Only the salt dissolves in the water. The heavier particles of sand and soil sink to the bottom of the jar. Filtering removes the smaller sand and soil particles. Finally, on the plate, the water *evaporates* to leave just the salt crystals.

Cabbage Detector

You can use cabbage water to test whether liquids are acids, *neutral*, or *alkaline*. Examples of acids are acetic acid (in vinegar) and citric acid (in oranges and lemons).

You will need

- Knife for chopping
- 2 glasses
- Heat-resistant bowls or jars
- White vinegar
- Baking soda
- Plastic dropper
- Boiling water
- Red cabbage

Step 1

Ask an adult to chop about two cupfuls of cabbage into small pieces. Place them in the bowl.

WARNING!
Ask an adult to help you with the hot water.

Step 2

Ask an adult to pour some boiling water into a bowl of red cabbage, then leave it for 15 minutes.

Step 3

Pour off the liquid into a bowl. This liquid is our "indicator."

Step 4

You need two known liquids to test your indicator. We are using white vinegar (acid) and a solution of baking soda in water (alkaline).

Step 5

Add indicator to your solution in drops. Watch the indicator color change. Wash the glasses thoroughly between tests.

Step 6

See where the results fall on this chart.

◄ more acidic   neutral   more alkaline ►

| red | purple | blue-violet | blue-green | green-yellow |

Try other kinds of colored vegetable juice to see if they make indicators.

How does it work?

The pigments or colors from the cabbage react with acids and alkalis to change the color. The juice should turn pink in acidic solutions and green in alkaline ones. Put some indicator drops in plain water. This is your neutral color. Use your indicator to test other liquids and compare the results.

Oil and Water

Some things don't get along well together. Take oil and water. These two can never be good friends, no matter how hard you try to mix or shake them together. If an oil tanker loses its oil at sea, a thick layer of crude oil sits on the surface of the water, causing problems for birds and fish. Oil from cars forms a greasy film on the top of puddles in the street. Even in a salad, the oil separates from the rest of the dressing. The scientific word for this is immiscible.

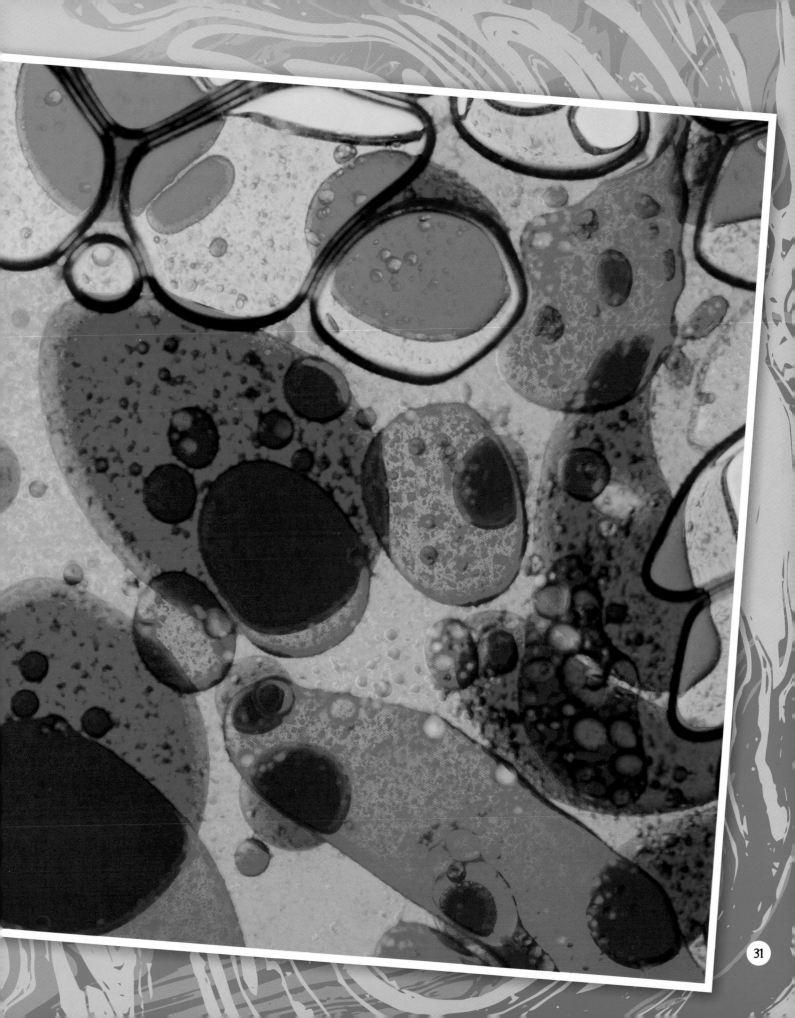

Color Storm

Oil and water don't mix. Or do they? In fact, milk contains both. Here's how you use oil and water to make a supercool pattern.

You will need

- 2 white plates
- Whole milk
- Dishwashing liquid
- A matchstick or skewer
- 3 or 4 colors of food coloring
- A notebook and pencil

Step 1

Pour water into a white plate. Wait for a minute or until the water stops moving.

Step 2

Put some evenly spaced drops of food coloring in the water.

Step 3

Pour some milk into the other plate. Wait for a minute for the milk to stop moving.

Step 4

Put some drops of food coloring in the milk, evenly spaced.

Step 5

Add one drop of dishwashing liquid to each of the plates.

Step 6

Look at your plates after a few minutes, then again after 10 minutes.

Step 7

Look at your plates again after 20 minutes. Use a notebook and pencil to write down the results.

Make notes of what you see:

- What happens when you add the food coloring to the water?

- What happens when you add the coloring to the milk?

- What happens when you add the dishwashing liquid to the water and milk?

- Keep reading to find out why ...

How does it work?

Milk is a special mixture of fat and water called an emulsion. The fat is not dissolved in the water, but the two are mixed together. (Cream at the top of milk is some of the fat that has separated.)

The food coloring doesn't travel through milk as easily as it does through water because it mixes with only the watery part of the milk.

When you add dishwashing liquid, two things happen. First, the surface tension of the water is destroyed. Then, the fat and water start to mix together because the dishwashing liquid breaks up the fat.

The movement of the food coloring shows you what's happening. It moves to the side of the saucer when the surface tension is broken, and it swirls in patterns as the fat and water start to mix together.

Secret Colors

Chromatography is a way of separating the parts that make up a mixture. We are going to use one type of chromatography, called paper chromatography, to find out what pigments make up different colored inks.

You will need

- **Colored felt-tip pens (not permanent or waterproof)**
- **Blotting paper**
- **A ruler**
- **Scissors**
- **Tape**
- **Bowl**
- **Water**
- **Pencil**
- **Notebook**

Step 1

Cut blotting paper into six strips, 6 x ½ in (100 x 15 mm).

Step 2

Number the strips and tape them to the ruler.

Step 3

Put a small dot of a different color on each strip, noting each strip number as the color is put on.

Step 4

Fill the bowl half full with water. Hang the strips over the edge of the bowl, so that the ends are just touching the water.

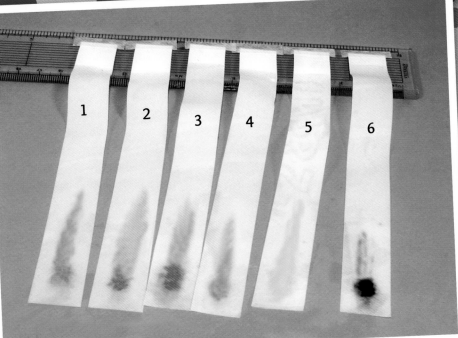

Step 5

Wait until the water is ¾ inch (20 mm) or so from the ruler, then remove the strips from the bowl, and record the colors you see. Sometimes a black will give a very surprising result!

How does it work?

Water moves up the strips by capillary action and carries the pigments with it. Some pigments are more strongly attracted to the paper fibers and so are not carried so far. A color may be made of many different pigments.

Invisible Ink

It's easy to send secret messages when you write them in top secret invisible ink! This is a supercool experiment to try with friends. The "secret" lies in the combination of lemon juice and heat from a light bulb or an iron. Let's try drawing a treasure map first!

You will need

- A toothpick
- A lemon
- A small knife
- Paper
- A bowl
- Heat source, such as a light bulb or iron

Step 1

Ask an adult to cut a lemon in half for you. Squeeze the lemon juice into a small bowl.

Step 2

The lemon juice is your "ink"! Dip the round end of a toothpick into the bowl.

WARNING!
Ask an adult to help you cut the lemon in half.

Step 3

Draw a secret map on some paper. Use lots of lemon juice for each part of the map you draw.

Step 4

Allow the paper to dry until you can't see the drawing anymore!

Step 5

Now move the paper back and forth under a heat source. As the lemon juice "ink" gets warm, your secret map is revealed.

How does it work?

The acid in the lemon juice breaks down the cellulose of the paper into sugars. The heat source tends to caramelize the sugars, making them brown and revealing your secret drawing.

Dense and Denser

If you take two similar-size cubes of wood and lead, the one made of lead would be much heavier. This is because lead is more dense than wood. It has more material packed into the same space.

You will need

- Glass jar
- 3 drinking glasses
- Various liquids: syrup, cooking oil, water
- Various solids: grape, coin, plastic wine cork
- Blue and red food coloring
- Plastic dropper

Experiment 1

Step 1

Gently pour the cooking oil, syrup, and water into a glass, one at a time.

cooking oil

water

syrup

Step 2

Let the liquids settle. They should form distinct layers.

PUSH AND PULL

In this chapter, we explore the science of forces. Forces are all around us and are acting on us all the time!

This man is skysurfing high above the Earth! This is made possible by the forces of gravity (pulling him down) and air resistance (slowing his fall).

Book Battle

This fantastic trick might seem like fiction, but actually it's all about friction!

You will need

- Two phone books or large catalogs with pages made of thin paper
- Two volunteers

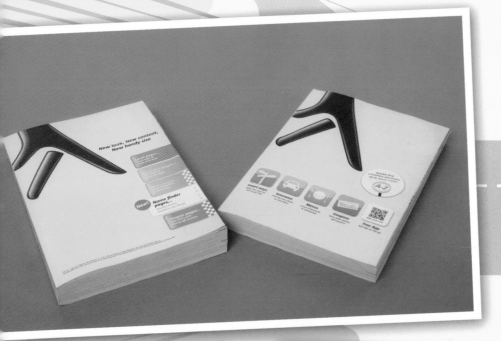

Step 1

Take two big, thick books, with plenty of pages.

Step 2

Turn a page from each book alternately, so that they overlap by an inch or two.

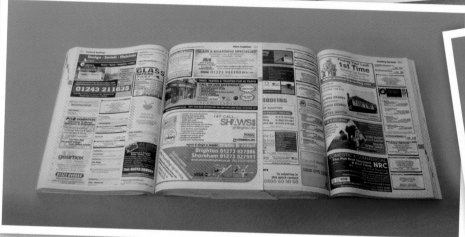

Step 4

Find two volunteers, and ask them whether they think they can pull the books apart. It looks easy—but in fact, it is impossible!

How does it work?

When you slide two pages across each other, a force called friction resists the movement. When all the pages of a book are overlapped as in our experiment, that friction is multiplied by the number of pages. That's a lot of friction—so it's actually impossible for anyone to pull the books apart!

Weird Water

This fiendishly clever bit of science can be used as a perfect practical joke to play on your friends and family!

You will need

- A plastic water bottle
- Water
- A thumbtack
- An outdoor space—this could get messy!

Step 1

Fill a plastic water bottle all the way up to the top.

Step 2

Screw the cap on firmly.

Step 3

Make holes around the sides of the bottle with a thumbtack. The water won't come out—yet! Now take your bottle somewhere that you don't mind getting wet.

Step 4

Ask a friend if they would like a drink of water, and hand them the bottle.

Step 5

When they open the lid ... the water will pour out of the holes. They're going to get soaked!

Try doing the same experiment with a soft-sided container, like a large plastic bag. Fill the bag with water, hold it up with one hand, and make holes with the thumbtack.

How does it work?

Water cannot escape through the holes while the lid is on, because the air pressure pushing on the side of the bottle is stronger than the downward pull of gravity on the water. But when the lid is removed, air rushes in and adds its force to gravity's pull ... and SPLASH!

Marble Madness

This experiment can be performed as a magic trick. Tell your family and friends that you are going to pick up a marble in a glass without touching the marble.

You will need

- A wine glass
- A marble
- A lot of patience and practice
- An audience to show the trick to!

Step 1

You will need a wine glass shaped like this.

This part is the bowl. It needs to be wider in the middle than at the rim.

Step 2

Ask a volunteer if they can pick up a marble without touching it or using the glass to scoop it up. They won't be able to!

Step 3

Now show them how it's done. Place the glass over the marble. Hold the glass by the base, and start gently moving it in a circular motion.

Step 4

The marble should start rolling around inside the glass.

Step 5

Rolling the marble at the right speed should keep it rotating in the widest part of the bowl. Lift the glass up as you rotate it. Your audience will be impressed!

How does it work?

This experiment is a contest between two forces: gravity and centrifugal force. As long as the marble is rolling fast enough, the centrifugal force pushing it outward to the widest part of the glass will be greater than the gravity pulling it downward. So the marble will roll around the glass rather than dropping out.

Balancing Butterfly

Is it possible to balance a piece of paper on a single finger? Sure it is! Here's how to make a beautiful, balancing butterfly.

You will need

- Thin cardstock
- Tracing paper
- Pins
- Scissors
- A black marker
- Colored markers or paints
- A pencil
- Small coins
- Superglue

Step 1

Draw a butterfly shape on a piece of thin cardstock. The tips of the wings must be above the head.

Step 2

Ink over the lines with a black marker. Decorate the body and wings with colored pens or paints.

Step 3

Cut out the shape with scissors.

Step 4

Glue matching coins to the tips of the wings.

Step 5

Bend the wings down a little.

Step 6

You should be able to balance the butterfly on the tip of your finger! The balance point should be near the head, depending on the weight of your coins and the cardstock thickness.

Step 7

You can put butterflies all around the room, on furniture, mirrors, ornaments, flowerpots—wherever there's a place for them to balance!

How does it work?

When the coin weights are added to the butterfly, the center of gravity falls almost directly between them, which is where your finger is, so it makes it easy to balance.

Under Pressure

The air around you has weight, and it presses down on everything it touches. That pressure is called atmospheric pressure. It is the force that is exerted on a surface by the air above it as gravity pulls it to Earth. However, water is much denser than air. A column of water that is 33 feet (10 meters) thick exerts the same pressure on a person as the entire Earth's atmosphere! Divers are careful not to descend too far, too quickly, since the pressure can be dangerous.

Step 3

Draw a face and body on the paper, like this. We're going to decorate this one as a fairy, but there are other ideas on page 58.

Draw your figure in the center of the paper.

Step 4

Roll the paper into a tube, overlapping as far as the pencil line. Fix it in place with the glue stick.

Step 5

Tape one half of the ball to each end. Finish drawing the top of the head.

Step 6

She won't stand up yet!

Step 7

Take the foot end off. Put a lump of modeling clay in the middle of the half ball, and stick it back on the body.

Step 8

Now stand your character up, and try pushing it over.

Step 9

You could make more wobblers and decorate them as aliens or circus performers—or use your own ideas!

How does it work?

The wobbler has a very low center of gravity, since its top half is light but the base is heavy. When another force acts on it (for instance, when you push it), gravity will pull it back to a point directly above the point where its mass is concentrated. This is called its state of equilibrium.

Parachute Jump

It's time to parachute some cork commandos behind enemy lines. Which parachute works best?

You will need

- String
- Materials for making the parachutes, such as plastic shopping bags, paper, tinfoil, and tissue paper
- A pencil and ruler
- Scissors
- Tape
- A cork
- A small eye hook
- A kitchen scale
- A sturdy chair
- A stopwatch (on a cell phone or watch)

Step 1

Using scissors, cut a 12 inch (30 cm) square from a plastic shopping bag.

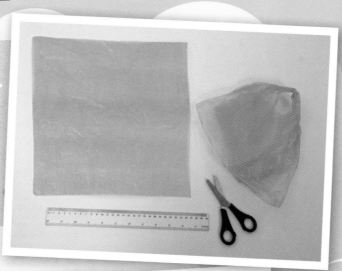

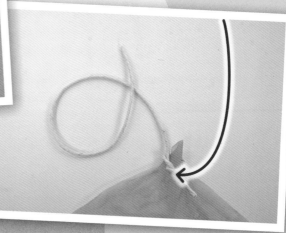

Step 2

Cut four pieces of string 30 cm (12 inches) long. Tie one end of each piece of string to a corner of the square of plastic.

Step 3

Twist an eye hook into one end of a cork.

Step 4

Hold the strings from the parachute together, and tie them to the screw.

Step 5

Stand on a chair, reach as high as you can, and drop the parachute.

Step 6

Try making parachutes of different sizes and materials. You can also try using other objects as weights, such as plastic toys. Drop them from the same height.

Step 7

Make a chart to see which features make the best parachutes. Time your test drops. Measure the size and weight of the parachute.

Size	Weight	Material	Time

How does it work?

Parachutes work by creating air resistance. This is a kind of friction that works against the pull of gravity. The best way to increase air resistance is to make as large a surface area as possible. So the size of your parachute will probably make more of a difference than anything else.

Out in Space

Astronauts wear spacesuits whenever they leave a spacecraft. In space, there is no air to breath, no air pressure, and it is very cold. Without protection, an astronaut would quickly die. When an astronaut gets out of a spacecraft while in space to do important tasks, it's called a spacewalk. A spacesuit keeps astronauts from getting too cold or hot, provides them with the water they need to drink, and supplies them with oxygen to breathe while working in space.

Down to Earth

All objects attract each other with gravity, and the larger the object, the larger the force. The Earth is huge so has a strong gravitational pull.

You will need

- A styrofoam cup
- Water
- A stepladder or something you can stand on safely
- An old ballpoint pen
- Small plastic bucket
- Somewhere outside to do the experiments

Experiment 1

Step 1

Make a small hole with the pen in the side of the cup near the base.

WARNING!
Ask an adult to help you when you're using the stepladder.

Step 2

Fill the cup with water. See how the water runs out.

Step 3

Cover the hole with your finger and fill the cup again. Stand on the stepladder, and drop the cup of water.

How does it work?

Gravity makes the cup and the water accelerate down at the same rate. They fall together, and the water stays in the cup until they hit the ground.

Experiment 2

Step 1

Half fill your bucket with water.

Step 2

Outside, swing the bucket forward and back. Increase the swing, and make sure you don't spill any water.

Step 3

When you get near the top of the swing, try going straight over the top in a complete circle!

How does it work?

When you swing the bucket, you apply a centrifugal force to the water in addition to gravity. The faster you swing, the greater the centrifugal force. When it's great enough, the water will stay in the bucket, regardless of gravity.

Jet Propulsion

Did you know that the first jet engine was invented in the first century AD? Find out how a jet engine works in this easy experiment.

You will need

- A sausage-shaped balloon
- A plastic straw
- Fishing line or fine string
- A bulldog clip
- Tape
- An empty juice carton
- Water
- Funnel
- An old ballpoint pen

Experiment 1

Step 1

Thread the fishing line or string through the straw.

Step 2

Find a big space, preferably outdoors. Fill the balloon with air, then put the bulldog clip on the neck to keep the air in.

Step 3

Fix the straw to the balloon with tape. Tie each end of the line to something fixed, at least 20 feet (6 m) apart.

Step 4

Release the clip!

How does it work?

The air inside the balloon is under pressure caused by the balloon trying to go back to its original shape. When the clip is released, air escapes through the neck, and the balloon is pushed in the opposite direction.

Experiment 2

Step 1

Open the top flaps of the fruit juice carton and make small holes in them. Attach a loop of string between the flaps and another to the exact middle of the first string.

Step 2

Make a hole in the front of the carton with the ballpoint pen, at the bottom on the left. Make a similar hole on the other side.

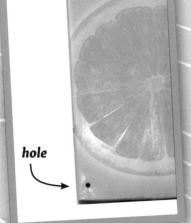

hole

Step 3

From here, it's best to work outside! Cover the holes with your finger and thumb, and fill the carton with water. You might need an assistant for this.

Step 4

Hold the carton up by the string, then uncover the holes.

How does it work?

The force of the escaping water on opposite sides drives the carton around in a circle, with the string acting as a pivot. We're using gravity and water to make jet propulsion!

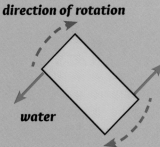

direction of rotation

water

Sink or Swim?

If we drop a piece of metal into water, it sinks. So how is it that a ship made of material that's heavier than water can float?

Experiment 1

Step 1

Knead a piece of plasticine into the size and shape of a golf ball.

Step 2

Fill the pitcher with water, then drop the clay ball into it. It sinks!

Step 3

Take the ball out of the water. Dry it, then form it into a hollow shape. Carefully lower the plasticine shape into the water again.

Step 4

Your boat will even carry cargo!

How does it work?

A ball of plasticine clay is denser than water, so in Step 2, it sinks. By spreading the clay out over a larger area, you are changing its density, so the plasticine in Step 3 floats.

Experiment 2

Step 1

Half fill the pitcher with water and add about six tablespoons of salt. Stir it well to dissolve the salt.

Step 2

Top up with plain water. Pour the water over a spoon so as not to mix it with the salt water.

Step 3

Carefully lower the egg into the glass using the spoon. Try not to disturb the water!

Step 4

The egg floats halfway down the pitcher!

How does it work?

The egg is denser than plain water but less dense than salt water. The egg has buoyancy in the salt water but not in the plain water, so it floats where the two kinds of water meet.

Thread Reel Racer

We store energy, such as gas, so it is available when we need it. Our bodies also take in forms of stored energy when we eat. Here's how to make a toy that uses stored energy move.

You will need

- A long pencil
- A rubber band
- An empty thread reel
- A piece of candle
- A paper clip
- A craft knife

Step 1

Get an adult to cut a slice of candle. Make a hole in the middle.

WARNING!
Ask an adult to cut the candle—don't do this yourself.

Step 2

Push the rubber band through the thread reel, then attach the paper clip.

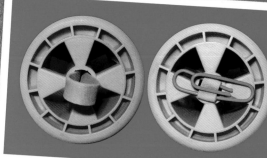

Step 3

Thread the rubber band through the candle.

BRIGHT IDEAS

In this chapter, we will explore the science surrounding the fastest thing in the universe—light! It travels at 186,000 miles (300,000 km) per second, in case you were wondering ...

This picture shows a "stellar nursery" far across our galaxy. This is where stars are born, and the light takes thousands of years to reach Earth. So when you are looking at the stars, you are actually looking at the past!

Kaleidoscope

Make thousands of crazy, colorful patterns with your own kaleidoscope!

You will need

- A paper towel tube
- A compass for drawing circles
- Paper
- Thin black cardstock
- A pen or pencil
- Mirrored cardstock
- A ruler
- Scissors
- Tape
- Colored tape
- A thumbtack
- Plastic wrap
- Tracing paper
- Small pieces of colored cellophane
- Colored wrapping paper

Step 1

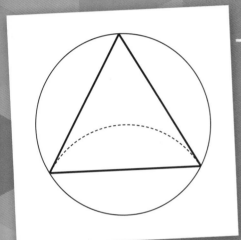

Draw around the bottom of a paper towel tube onto a piece of paper. Open your compass so the point is on the circle and the pencil is exactly in the middle. Draw the shape shown with dotted lines. Mark in the base of the triangle. Open your compass to this line, then mark the third point of your triangle. Draw the triangle.

Step 2

Using a ruler, draw a rectangle the same length as the cardboard tube on the back of the mirror cardstock. Mark off three parts with the same width as the sides of the triangle you drew.

Step 3

Fold the mirror cardstock along the lines to form a triangular shape. The mirrored side should be on the inside. Slide it into the paper towel tube.

Step 4

Draw around the end of the tube onto a piece of black cardstock. Cut out the circle, using scissors.

Step 5

Stick the circle on the end of the tube with tape. Make a hole in the center.

Step 6

Turn over the tube. Stretch plastic wrap over this end, and fix it in place with tape.

Step 7

Cut a 1 inch- (25 mm-) wide strip of thin cardstock, and tape it around the end of the tube. Make sure it stands out a little from the end of the tube.

Step 8

Place some small pieces of colored cellophane on top of the plastic wrap.

Step 9

Draw around the bottom of the tube onto tracing paper. Cut out the circle, leaving a gap of about half an inch (1 cm). Cut small flaps around the edge. Place this shape over the top of the tube, then stick down the flaps with tape.

Step 10

Decorate the tube with wrapping paper.

Step 11

Hold your kaleidoscope up to the light. Look through the hole and turn the tube. What do you see?

How does it work?

Light normally travels in a straight line. When it hits a mirror, it bounces off it in a different direction—this is called reflection. In a kaleidoscope, the light bounces around back and forth off the walls, creating many, many reflections of the colorful objects inside.

Hall of Mirrors

Have you ever been to the fair and looked in the carnival mirrors? They can make you look tall, short, wide or just plain weird! Here's how to make your own.

You will need

- A big shiny spoon
- 2 shallow cardboard boxes (e.g., shoebox lids)
- Four sheets of thin mirror cardstock
- Tape
- Scissors
- A craft knife
- Adhesive putty
- Thin black cardstock

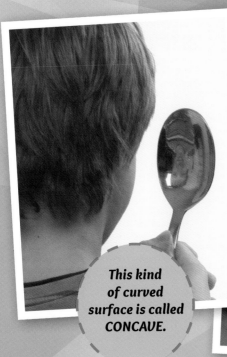

This kind of curved surface is called CONCAVE.

This kind of curved surface is called CONVEX.

Step 1

Look at your reflection in a shiny spoon. What differences can you see between the reflections on each side?

Step 2

Let's make some mirrors to see those effects more clearly! Line the sides of a shallow cardboard box with black cardstock. Strengthen the corners with tape.

Step 3

Measure the inside of your box. Then cut a piece of thin mirror cardstock or plastic to the same width as the box but about 2 inches (5 cm) longer.

Step 4

Bend the mirror and place it in the box. The sides should hold it securely.

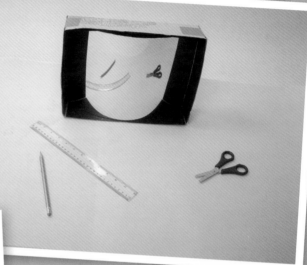

Step 5

Cut a hole in the bottom of another box with scissors, leaving half an inch (12 mm) around the edge.

Step 6

Prepare the mirror cardstock as before, but this time turn it the other way up.

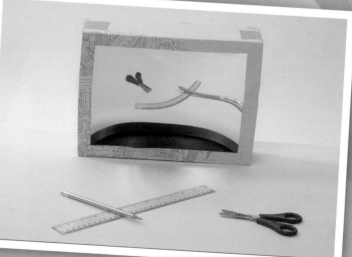

3-D Glasses

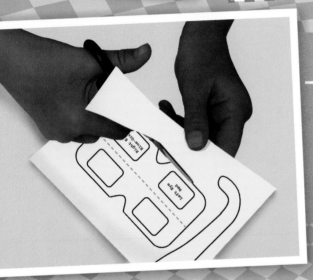

View amazing 3-D pictures through your own handmade glasses!

You will need

- **Cardstock or cardboard**
- **Red and blue-green colored plastic (called Mylar) from a craft store**
- **Tape**
- **A glue stick**
- **Scissors**
- **The 3-D images on pages 90–91**

Step 1

Copy the template opposite, and cut out the three parts of the glasses. Score along the dotted lines.

Step 2

Cut out two rectangles of colored plastic—one should be blue-green and the other red. Tape them to the glasses.

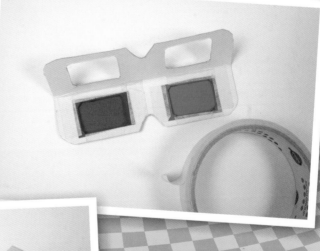

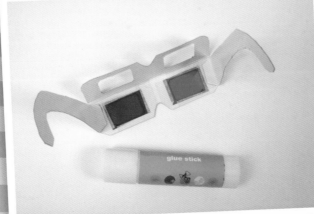

Step 3

Fold the earpiece flaps along the dotted lines and fix to the frame with a glue stick or tape.

Step 4

Fold the frame down to seal in the lenses and the earpiece flaps. Secure them with tape.

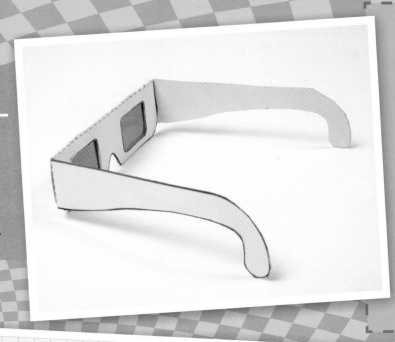

How does it work?

The blue-green lens makes it hard to see blue and green, but you can still see red. The red lens does the opposite. Your brain tries to make sense of the different images each eye is seeing by turning them into a 3-D picture!

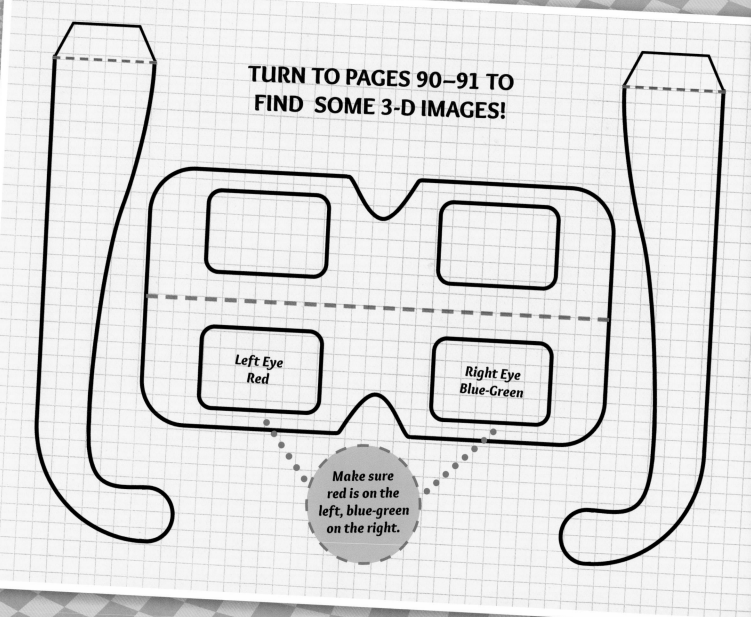

TURN TO PAGES 90–91 TO FIND SOME 3-D IMAGES!

Left Eye Red

Right Eye Blue-Green

Make sure red is on the left, blue-green on the right.

Put on your glasses and look at these pictures.

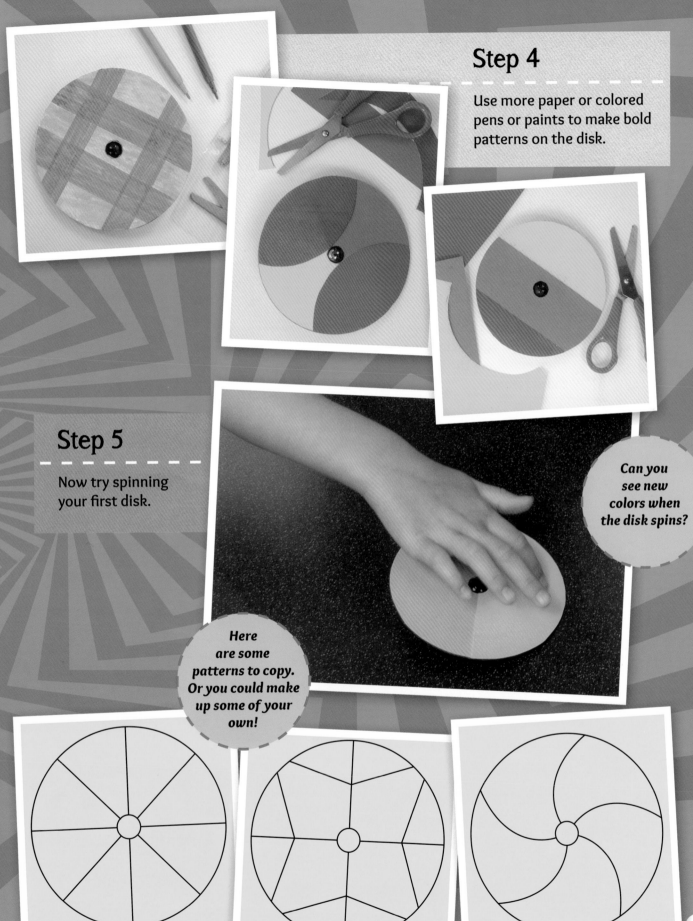

Step 4

Use more paper or colored pens or paints to make bold patterns on the disk.

Step 5

Now try spinning your first disk.

Can you see new colors when the disk spins?

Here are some patterns to copy. Or you could make up some of your own!

Step 6

Here's a way to make neat segments. Fold a circle three times. Then cut along the last fold with the scissors.

What happens if you make a spiral pattern?

How does it work?

When the top whirls around really fast, you can see all the colors, but your brain can't separate them. So what you see is a blend of all the colors mixed together.

Make Your Own Zoetrope

Have you ever dreamed of being an animator? You can make a start here by creating your first-ever moving picture!

You will need

- A circular box (such as a cheese box) with a lid
- Modeling clay
- A map tack
- A small button
- A piece of cork
- Tape
- A ruler
- Scissors
- A pencil and pen
- Black paper and white paper
- Colored paper

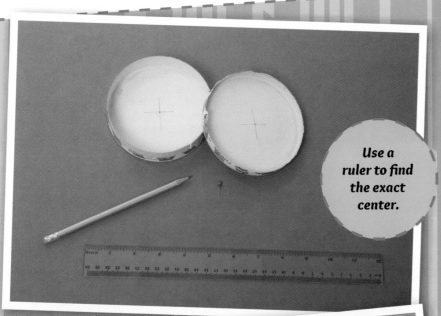

Use a ruler to find the exact center.

Step 1

Poke a hole in the center of a circular box and its lid with a map tack.

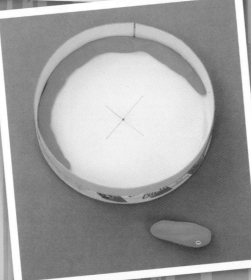

Step 2

Put some modeling clay around the edge of the inside of the box, to add weight.

Step 3

Push the map tack through the lid, through the hole in a button, through the bottom of the base, and into a cork beneath. The box should now spin freely on the lid.

Step 4

Cut a piece of black paper about 2.5 inches (6.5 cm) high that will fit around the inside edge of the lid.

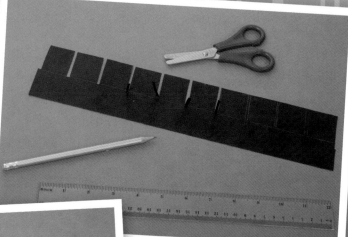

Step 5

Draw lines along the black paper about 1 inch (3 cm) apart. Following those guidelines, cut slots about 1.5 inches (4 cm) deep.

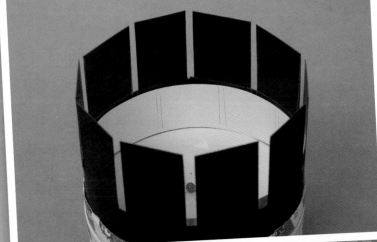

Step 6

Stick the black paper in place with tape. Then cut a piece of white paper, 1¼ inches (3 cm) wide to fit inside it. Don't stick it down yet!

A repeated action that joins up at the beginning and end will work well.

Step 7

Draw guidelines along the white paper 1¼ inches (3 cm) apart. Draw a series of pictures in the "frames" that you have marked out. Put the paper inside the box.

Step 8

Spin the zoetrope and watch your animation through the slits.

You could decorate the outside of the box with colored paper.

How does it work?

When you spin the zoetrope, you can see each of the pictures one at a time in very quick succession. Your brain tries to make sense of what your eyes take in. It interprets these rapidly changing pictures as movement, so you see a continuous moving picture.

Rainbow Maker

You don't need to wait for rain to see a rainbow anymore. Here is how to make a nice, dry one indoors. You may not find a pot of gold at the end, though!

You will need

- Some old CDs
- A sunny day, or if this is not possible, a flashlight
- A window with curtains or blinds
- White paper

Step 1

Find a sunny window. Close the blind or curtain, but leave a little gap to let the direct sunlight in.

Step 2

Hold a CD, shiny side up, in the beam of sunlight.

Step 3

Reflect the light onto a piece of white paper.

Step 4

Change the angle of the CD. You will see a variety of different rainbow patterns.

Step 5

You can use a flashlight if it's not a sunny day, but the rainbows might not be as bright.

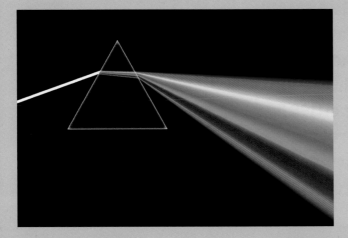

How does it work?

When white light passes through a triangular prism, it splits into all the different colors of the rainbow. The surface of a CD is made of plastic with lots of tiny ridges above a mirrored surface. These act like lots of tiny prisms arranged in a circle, so when light hits the surface of the CD, it makes a rainbow.

Night Lights

Before the invention of the electric light, the Earth would have looked very different at night from how it looks now. This image is a satellite picture of Earth from space taken at night. It shows a clear outline of the United States.

The brightest lights show us where the major cities and towns are. Cities tend to grow up along coastlines and transportation networks, such as rivers, roads, and railroads.

Pepper's Ghost

This experiment is part science and part magic trick, and all about not necessarily believing what we see. The effect is named after John Pepper, the nineteenth-century scientist who perfected it. We are going to reveal the secret of Pepper's ghost ...

You will need

- A cardboard box—about 12 x 9 x 15 inches (30 x 22 x 40 cm)
- Tape
- Sheets of strong black paper
- Clear plastic—the same size as one face of box
- A tea light with holder
- Matches
- Cardboard tube—about 3 in (8 cm) diameter, 6 in (15 cm) tall
- A sheet of cardstock
- A glass of water
- Glue stick
- Paints and brushes

Step 1

Measure 1 inch (3 cm) in from the edges of one side of the box, then cut a window.

Step 2

Using the glue and tape, line the inside of the box with black paper, except for the window. Fix the plastic over the window with tape.

Step 3

Ask an adult to help you cut a piece out of the cardboard tube, about a quarter of its *circumference*, from top to base. Line the inside of the rest of the tube with black paper.

Step 4

Light the tea light and place it in front of the box. Fill the glass with water. Find the position of the virtual image of the tea light, and put the glass inside the box.

Step 5

Position the tube so that the candle is totally screened from the front.

Step 6

Now view the effect from the front. The candle should seem to be still burning underwater!

How does it work?

Normally, we can see straight through clear plastic, and in daylight, it appears as if all the light goes through. In fact, a small amount is reflected, but in daylight, it's too faint to see.

In this experiment, we've positioned the glass so that the candle's reflection in the plastic is in the exact same place. This optical illusion tricks your brain into thinking that the candle is burning underwater.

Light Trap

This experiment shows you how fiber optics works. Light can only travel in straight lines, but it's possible to bounce it inside of a material like water. You can use this technique to make it travel along a stream of water!

You will need

- A glass or glass container
- Water
- A little milk
- A plastic bottle
- Tin foil
- A kitchen sink
- Flashlight
- Tape
- A small screwdriver
- A friend to help you
- A kitchen you can make dark

Experiment 1

Step 1

Fill a glass container with water. Add a few drops of milk.

Step 2

Put some tin foil around the end of your flashlight, then make a slit in it.

Step 3

Darken the room. With the slit horizontal, shine the flashlight up through the side of the glass, adjusting the angle until light reflects down from the surface of the water.

Step 3

Carefully cut three sides of the flap and fold inward. Use tape to fix the flap at a 45° slant.

Step 4

Cut a flap at the top of the box on the other side, the same size (X by X) as before. Fix this flap, again at a 45° slant, with tape.

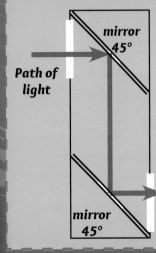

Step 5

Stick one mirror to each flap with some glue.

Step 6

Now test your periscope!

How does it work?

mirror 45°

Path of light

mirror 45°

Light travels in straight lines. The first mirror changes the direction of the light by reflecting it. Then, the second mirror changes it back, parallel to its original path. Submarines use periscopes so that the crew can see above the waves while the submarine remains safely under the water.

111

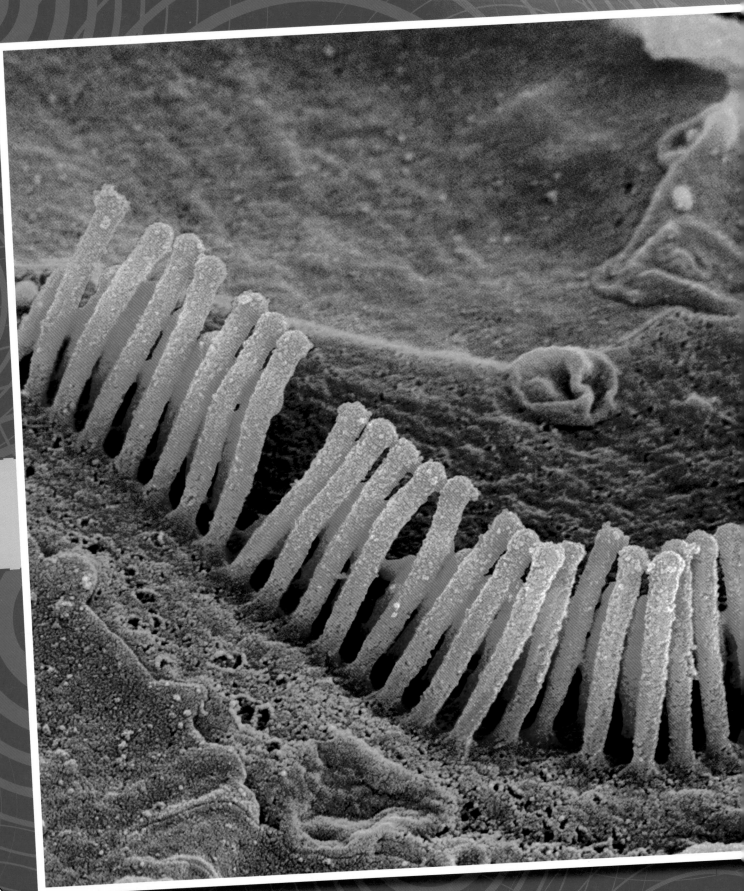

SUPER SONIC

Did you know that everything you hear is a vibration? Get ready to learn about the science of sound!

This photo shows the inside of an ear that has been magnified 21,000 times! Sound vibration makes the liquid in the inner ear move in waves, which makes the hairs sway. Then they turn that movement into an electrical signal, which is sent to your brain!

Make Your Own Drum Set

March to the beat of your own drum with this noisy experiment. Using household objects, you can create a drum set that works just like the real thing!

You will need

- Containers such as small glass jars, cans, and plastic buckets
- Materials to make the drum skins, such as plastic shopping bags, paper, cloth, tin foil, and balloons
- Materials to make drumsticks, such as chopsticks, skewers, and wooden spoons
- A metal saucepan lid
- Some string
- Rubber bands
- Marker pens
- Scissors
- Tape
- A glue stick
- Colorful paper

Which containers and drum skins work the best?

Step 1

Draw around a can onto a plastic shopping bag. Then cut out the circle with scissors, adding a half-inch (10 mm) margin around the edge.

Step 2

Stick the sheet in place with pieces of tape, pulling the skin tight as you go. Then decorate the can by gluing on colored paper.

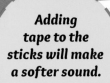

Adding tape to the sticks will make a softer sound.

Step 3

Test your first drum with two drumsticks!

115

Step 4

Cut down one side of a balloon with a pair of scissors, to make a stretchy skin. Pull it over the top of a small container. Hold it in place with a rubber band.

The rubber band should be tight.

Step 5

Make some more drums from other materials. Each should sound slightly different. Finally, make a cymbal by tying a string around the knob on a saucepan lid. Hang it above the rest of your drum set.

How does it work?

When you hit a drum, it creates a vibration, which is what we hear as a noise. Lots of different things can change the pattern of the vibrations, which changes the noise that you hear: the materials you use, the size of the drum, how tight the skin is stretched, and even where you hit it.

Paper Popper

Who knew that a piece of paper could be so loud?

You will need

- A sheet of paper measuring 16 x 12 inches (40 x 30 cm)

Step 1

Fold the paper in half along the long side, then open it out again.

Step 2

Fold the corners into the crease line in the middle, like this.

Step 3

Fold it again along the original central crease.

117

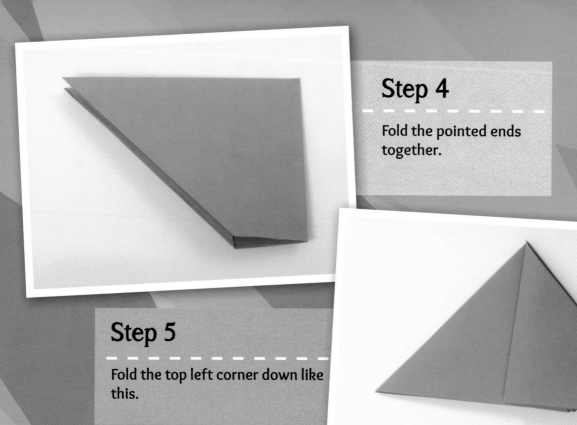

Step 4

Fold the pointed ends together.

Step 5

Fold the top left corner down like this.

Step 6

Turn it over, and fold the flap down in the same way on the other side.

Step 7

The paper should look like this.

Hold this end!

1

Step 8

Hold the noisemaker like this.

Step 9

Swing the noisemaker down like this. It should make a sound like cracking a whip!

2

3

How does it work?

Swinging the noisemaker downward compresses (squashes) the air inside it. The air is suddenly freed when the inner fold opens out. That causes a rapid decompression: a small explosion of air!

119

Dancing Flame

We all know you can make a flame flutter by blowing on it, but did you know that you can make a flame dance with the power of sound?

Step 1

Using scissors, cut the bottom off a plastic bottle.

WARNING!
Ask an adult to help you cut the bottom off the plastic bottle.

Step 2

Cut a square of plastic from a plastic bag that is at least half an inch (1 cm) bigger than the base of the bottle. Fix it to the base with a rubber band.

Step 3

Light the candle. Position the bottle so that the neck points toward the flame.

Step 4

Tap the plastic sheet without moving the bottle. The candle flame will flicker with the sound!

How does it work?

All sounds are vibrations in the air. We don't normally see what is happening when the air vibrates—we just hear it as the vibrations reach our ears. However, the small flame in our experiment is so sensitive to air movement, that we can clearly see it move in response to vibrations traveling through the air.

What a Noise!

When an object vibrates, it causes movement in the air particles called sound waves. These particles bump into the particles close to them, which makes them vibrate, too, causing them to bump into more air particles. This movement keeps going until they run out of energy. If your ear is in range of the vibrations, you hear the sound. The howler monkey shown here on the right is known for its extremely loud howls, which can travel 3 miles (5 km) through dense rain forest.

Funky Bone Vibrations

We already know that vibrations can travel through air. They can also travel through other materials, such as ... your head!

You will need

- A fork
- A table or a hard surface

Step 1

Bang the fork on a table so that it makes a ringing noise.

Don't risk damaging an expensive table— any hard surface will do.

Step 2

Note how loud the noise is.

Secret Sounds

Sound travels to our ears through the air by making the molecules in the air vibrate, but it can also pass through solid materials in the same way. We are going to show that sound can pass through solid materials.

You will need

- A friend to help you
- String
- Metal objects such as silverware or a coat hanger
- 2 clean yogurt cups
- Hammer
- Nail

Experiment 1

Step 1

Tie the ends of two pieces of string to metal objects.

Step 2

Hold the end of the string and gently put your finger in your ear. Swing the object so that it bangs against a wall. Now try using both objects.

How does it work?

When the object is hit, it vibrates, making a sound that we can hear normally. As we are suspending the objects on taut string, the vibration will travel up the string, making it vibrate. Because we have our fingers pressed into our ears, we can't hear normally through the air, but we can hear the transmitted vibration coming up the string.

IT'S ALIVE

The world is full of fascinating and amazing living things. The area of science that looks at living things is called biology.

Honeybees are fascinating creatures. They use an expressive "waggle dance" to tell other bees the direction and distance of good sources of food.

Growing Seeds

You will need

- Paper towel
- Thick cardboard
- 4 clean, shallow food trays
- Quick-germinating seeds, such as alfalfa
- Water
- A refrigerator

Many plants spread themselves by scattering seeds. A seed contains a new plant and enough food for it to start growing. We are going to find out what else a seed needs to germinate—water, light, warmth? You'll need to collect some food trays for this project.

Step 1

Put three or four thicknesses of paper towel in the bottom of each tray. Scatter the same number of seeds in each tray. Label them A, B, C, D. Wet the paper towels in trays A, B, and C.

A *has water, light, and warmth*

B *has no warmth and no light*

C *has no light*

D *has no water*

compost   sand   gravel   soil

Step 3

After a week, you should be able to see clearly which plants are thriving or failing. Do you know why?

compost

Step 4

Remove the BEST plant from the jar to check the root structure. Notice that both the leaves and the roots are developing well. This plant likes the conditions you have provided.

How does it work?

Results should prove that plants prefer a mixed material to grow in, such as garden soil or compost. They will not grow as well in sand or gravel, which provides no nutrients.

Step 5

Remove the WORST plant from the jar to check the root structure. The plant is weak. Notice that both the leaves and the roots are not developing well. This plant does not like the conditions you have provided.

gravel

151

Stone Flowers

These unusual plants are known as living stones, stone flowers, or pebble plants. They are one of the world's most fascinating plants! They look so much like the pebbles and stones among which they grow in Africa, that they were only discovered by scientists in 1811.

DNA from Strawberries

DNA is the thing that makes you YOU. It is found in every one of your cells and contains the instructions that your body has followed to make you the way you are. Every living creature has different DNA. Now you can see the DNA of strawberries in your very own kitchen!

You will need

- A freezer
- 3 strawberries
- Salt
- A measuring cup
- Scissors
- Paper towel
- A plastic bag
- 2 plastic cups
- Laundry detergent (liquid or powdered)
- A glass
- Ice cubes
- 2 big bowls
- A fork
- A teaspoon
- A toothpick
- Ice-cold rubbing alcohol (ask an adult for help)

Step 1

Put the rubbing alcohol in the freezer at least an hour before you do this experiment.

Step 2

Remove the stems from the strawberries, then break them up using a fork.

Step 3

Put the pieces into a measuring cup. Add one teaspoon of detergent to half a cup of warm water, and pour the mixture over the fruit.

Step 4

Stand the cup in a bowl of warm water. The detergent and warm water will start breaking up the strawberry cells. Wait 12 minutes, stirring often.

Step 5

Next, stand the cup in a bowl of ice cubes for 5 minutes.

Step 6

Cut the corner off the plastic bag and line it with the paper towel. Then pour the strawberry mush through, so that the liquid with the DNA collects in a cup.

Step 7

Add a quarter teaspoon of salt to the collected liquid. Mix it well.

Step 8

Now pour some of the mixture into a clear glass, so it is about a third full. Ask an adult to pour in an equal amount of ice-cold rubbing alcohol, and then rock the glass gently.

Step 9

Let the glass stand for a few minutes. A cloudy patch should form at the top of the mixture. It may look bubbly or whitish. This is strawberry DNA! You can remove it with a toothpick. It will look like clear slime! Isn't it incredible to think that the slime contains all the information for making a strawberry plant?

How does it work?

To get to a strawberry's DNA, first we mash the fruit to break open its cells. Then we separate the cells into their parts, using the enzymes in laundry detergent. The ice stops the detergent from breaking apart the DNA itself. Then we filter the mixture, and the liquid we are left with is called the "supernatent," which contains the DNA. Finally, adding salt and rubbing alcohol makes the DNA break apart from the rest of the solution and rise to the top.

Ready for My Close-Up

Scientists use a special piece of equipment called a microscope to look at things very closely. Like a magnifying glass, it makes small objects appear much larger. This photo shows a close-up of the scales on a blue morpho butterfly. Its wings are covered in bright blue-and-green shimmery scales. These scales reflect light differently depending on its direction.

Step 3

Put the smaller bowl in the bigger bowl. Add water to the smaller bowl until it is ¾ full.

Step 4

Hold the bottle in the bowl with the neck in the water, then take off the cap.

Keep the neck of the bottle under the water!

Step 5

Put the end of the straw in the bottle. Blow out one big breath!

Step 6

You will be able to see how much air you can store in your lungs! Ask a friend or family member to try the experiment. Who has the biggest lung capacity?

How does it work?

When you blow down, the air you breath out forces out the water that was in the bottle. The empty space is exactly equal to how much air your lungs can hold.

Seeing Things

So far, we have experimented with some of the living things in the world around us. But we are alive, too, and we can also experiment on ourselves! We are going to learn a little about how our eyes work and how using two eyes is often better than one!

You will need

- Small table
- Large sheet of paper
- 3 different-colored markers
- A jar lid
- Scissors
- Thin cardstock
- A pencil
- Glue stick
- String

Experiment 1

Step 1

Draw a target on paper, and put it flat on a table.

Step 2

COVER ONE EYE. To test your aim, hold a marker with the top removed, at arm's length. Try to drop it on the center of the target.

COVER THE OTHER EYE. Repeat the test, and try to hit the target with the next marker.

USE BOTH EYES. Repeat test with last marker.

HOT STUFF

Temperature can completely change the behavior of the materials around us, or in some cases, it can transform them completely. It's time to learn about the science of hot and cold!

Did you know that hot air is lighter than cold air? That is how a hot-air balloon flies!

Hot Topic: Conduction

Conduction is the way heat is carried through solid materials, for example, from a stove burner through the saucepan to the food. We are going to find out which materials are best at conducting heat.

Step 1

Ask an adult to help you heat some water.

WARNING!
Ask an adult to help you with boiling water.

Step 2

Put some hot water in the mug. Be careful!

182

Step 3

Stand the first object in the water. Hold the other end. See how long it takes to become warm.

Step 4

Fill the mug with hot water again, and try other things. This time we're testing a metal coat hanger.

Step 5

Now it's a plastic drinking straw.

Step 6

This is a wooden spoon.

How does it work?

Energy in the form of heat passes from one molecule to the next along the object. Metals conduct heat well and so are called good conductors. Nonmetals, like plastics and wood, are not good conductors and are called insulators.

Moving Story: Convection

The way that heat is carried through liquids and gases is called convection. An example of this is a radiator heating up a whole room. We are going to show a convection current in air by using smoke.

You will need

- Shoebox with a lid
- 2 paper towel tubes
- Tealight candle in a holder
- An ice pop stick
- Tape
- Scissors
- Thin cardstock
- Matches
- Thread

Step 1

Draw two circles on the lid of the shoebox, one toward each end. Draw around the end of the paper towel tube.

Step 2

Cut the holes out, and stick the tubes in place with tape.

Step 3

Light the tealight candle. Put it in the shoebox, so that it is under one of the tubes when the lid goes on.

Step 4

Light the end of the ice pop stick with a match. (Ask an adult to help.) Then blow the flame out.

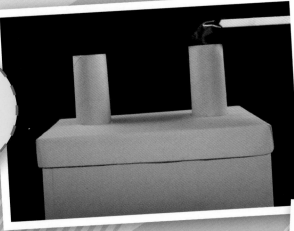

Step 5

Hold the glowing stick over the tube that doesn't have the tealight under it.

Step 6

Smoke goes down the tube and eventually comes out of the other. Make sure you blow out the candle once the experiment is over!

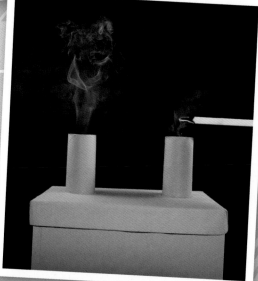

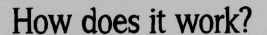

How does it work?

The candle flame heats the air, which rises up through the tube. Cooler air is heavier and is drawn down the other tube. Air travels through the box, drawing the smoke with it.

185

Warming Glow: Radiation

Radiation is the only form of heat that can travel through a vacuum. An example is the way heat gets to us from the sun, through space. The heat we feel from a desk lamp is also radiation. We are going to show how different substances absorb heat radiation.

Experiment 1

Step 1

Find a place to work where the temperature is fairly even. Keep away from direct sunlight and room heaters. Note the room temperature.

Step 2

We are using a desk lamp as a source of radiant heat. Put your thermometer under the lamp. Note the temperature rise after ten minutes.

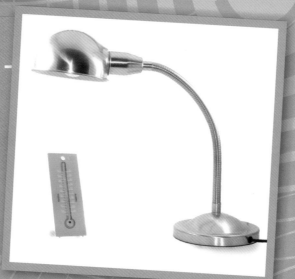

How does it work?

Heat is getting to the thermometer by radiation. It is a way in which heat travels as waves of energy.

Disappearing Act

When we put certain things like salt or sugar into water, they seem to disappear. In fact, they are still there but have dissolved. We are going to see how temperature affects dissolving.

You will need

- Salt
- Small saucepan
- Two spoons
- Thermometer
- Water and stove
- Measuring cup

Step 1

Pour 16 fluid ounces (500 ml) of cold water into a measuring cup.

Step 2

Pour the water into a saucepan. Add salt, one spoonful at a time.

Step 3

Use another spoon to stir the water. Count how many spoonfuls can be added before no more will dissolve.

Step 4

Pour out the salty water. Now add a pint (500 ml) of warm water to the saucepan. Repeat with the water at different temperatures, using the same quantity of water and same size spoon each time.

See if the same thing happens with other solids. You could try different kinds of sugar, sand, or even chalk dust!

How does it work?

The hotter the water, the more salt it can hold in solution. When you let the water cool, the salt cannot stay in solution, and it falls out as salt crystals on the bottom of the pan.

sand

white sugar

crushed chalk

brown sugar

203

Mini Melt

In this chilly experiment, you can create a miniature iceberg to see how the density of water changes with temperature.

You will need

- Water
- A measuring cup
- A glass
- Food coloring
- 1/3 cup of vegetable oil
- An ice cube tray
- A freezer

Step 1

Prepare some special ice cubes by adding a few drops of food coloring to some water in a measuring cup.

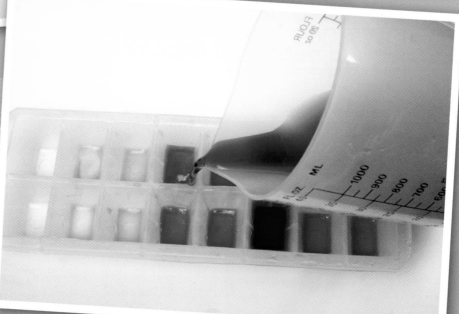

Step 2

Fill an ice cube tray with the colored water. Put it in the freezer. It should be frozen in 2 to 3 hours.

Step 7

Pat down the foil envelope with the oven glove, then let it cool.

Step 8

When it is cool, remove the shrunken bag from inside.

Step 9

Make gifts for your friends! Attach a brooch pin to the back of the miniature bags to make buttons.

How does it work?

The molecules making up the bag are in long chains called polymers, which are knotted tightly together. When the bag was made, it was heated and the polymers were stretched out flat. Heating up the empty bag releases the polymers, so they can scrunch up again.

Sun Burst

The sun is almost 93 million miles (145 million km) from the Earth. Without the sun, there would be no life on Earth. But get too close to this gigantic ball of fire, and you'll burn up! The sun often releases large amounts of gas into its atmosphere. These are known as solar flares. Some solar flares can be truly massive and contain impressive power. Sometimes, these powerful flares can even damage satellites orbiting the earth.

Solar Still

If you were ever stranded in the wilderness, this cool experiment could save your life by creating drinkable water from salt water!

You will need

- A sunny day!
- A large bowl
- A small jar or glass
- Plastic wrap
- A pitcher of water
- Salt
- A tablespoon
- Small, clean stones or marbles

Step 1

Put salt in a pitcher of water. Add about 4 tablespoons of salt to 1 quart (1 liter) of water. Stir thoroughly.

Step 2

Pour enough salty water into a large bowl so that it is about 2 inches (5 cm) deep.

Step 3

Place the small jar or glass in the center of the bowl of water. Make sure the top of the jar is above the salt water but well below the top of the large bowl. You'll probably need to put some small, clean stones or marbles in the glass to weigh it down and stop it from floating in the water.

Step 4

Stretch some plastic wrap over the top of the large bowl and make an airtight seal.

Step 5

Place a marble in the center of the plastic wrap, directly over the jar, to make it slope down into the middle.

Step 6

Put your solar still outside in the sun. Leave it for at least 4 hours. The longer you leave it out, the more water you'll collect.

Step 7

When you are ready to check your solar still, take off the plastic wrap and look at the water that's collected in the jar. Do you think it's salty or fresh? Taste it and see!

How does it work?

The heat from the sun causes water to evaporate from the bowl, leaving the salt behind. As this happens, the water vapor hits the plastic wrap and condenses back into liquid water again. The marble weighing the plastic down makes the water run down into the jar, thereby allowing you to collect fresh water!

Feeling Hot and Cold

Why is it that people feel temperature differently? When some people are snuggled up in coats, other people are walking around in T-shirts. This experiment tests how this is possible.

You will need

- 2 small containers, e.g., plastic pails
- A large bowl
- Hot water
- Cold water
- Ice cubes
- Room temperature water
- A towel

Step 1

Pour cold water and ice cubes into a bucket.

Step 2

Pour hot (not boiling) water into another bucket.

Step 7

Your oven is ready—let's make a tasty treat! Put a cookie on a paper plate and cover with marshmallows and chocolate.

Step 8

Check on progress in the oven every 10 minutes. Make sure sunlight is still reflected into the oven. On a nice, sunny day, it should take about 30 minutes.

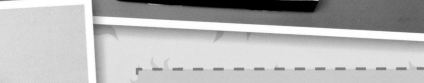

How does it work?

The idea of a solar oven is to capture as much of the sun's heat as possible. The color black absorbs heat, so this makes sure that the cooking area of the box soaks up as much warmth as possible. Silver reflects heat, so the lid is used to gather more of the sun's heat and direct it to the food. The plastic wrap acts like glass in a greenhouse, allowing the light and heat in but not letting it out again. All three together make a pretty good oven!

Soap Sculptures

Create your own fun soap sculptures just using the microwave!

You will need

- **2 or 3 bars of luxury soap**
- **A microwave oven**
- **An oven glove**
- **Paper plates**
- **Plastic lids from aerosol cans**

Step 1

Put a bar of soap on a paper plate. Ask an adult to put it in the microwave on a high setting for 1 minute.

WARNING!
Ask an adult to help you use the microwave.

Step 2

Watch through the closed door of the microwave. The soap should expand and grow!

How does it work?

We've connected the bulbs together in the circuit like a daisy chain. This is called a series circuit. Every bulb we add to the circuit increases the energy required for the electricity to flow.

Lamps in series

Experiment 2

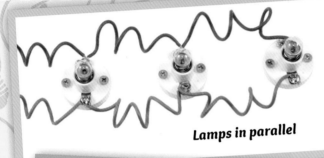

Lamps in parallel

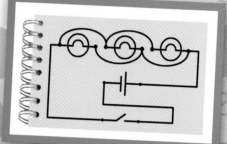

There's another way to use electricity in a circuit, in parallel. Let's see what difference it makes to the result.

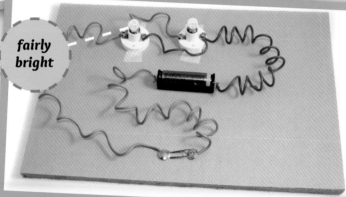

fairly bright

Step 1

Start as in Step 1, page 238. Connect one more lamp in the way shown above, using two more wires. Turn it on.

Step 2

Turn it off, then connect a third lamp with two more wires, as in the diagram above. Turn it on again.

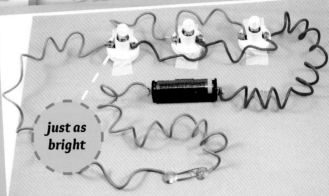

just as bright

How does it work?

This time, we've connected the lamps in parallel. Each bulb in the circuit gets the right amount of electricity to make it work. The battery might not last for long running three bulbs, though.

239

Lightning Strikes!

Lightning is a flash of electricity that is produced during a thunderstorm. All thunderstorms produce lightning and are very dangerous. Lightning is an electric current. Within a thundercloud way up in the sky, small pieces of ice (frozen raindrops) bump into each other as they move around in the air. All of those little collisions make an electric charge. After a while, the whole cloud fills up with electrical charges, and lightning lights up the sky.

The Lemon Battery

When you get tired of buying fresh batteries for your experiments, here's a way of making your own. The trouble is, you may have to buy some lemons instead! We are going to produce electricity and power a device using fresh fruit!

You will need

- 3 ice pop sticks
- Tin foil (this is really made of aluminum)
- 3 lemons
- 8 paper clips
- 3 pieces of copper tube about 4 inches long (10 cm)
- Insulated wire
- An old calculator with an LCD
- Small knife

WARNING!
Ask an adult to help you cut the holes in the lemons.

Step 1

Get an adult to cut a square hole and a slot in each lemon with a small knife.

Step 2

Wrap the ice pop sticks with tin foil, and push one into the slot of each lemon.

Step 3

Push one piece of copper tube into each lemon.

Step 4

Use paper clips to attach the wires.

Step 5

Ask an adult to open your calculator, remove the battery, and reveal the terminals. This calculator has a red wire marked "+" and a black wire marked "−."

WARNING!
Ask an adult to help you with steps 5 and 6.

How does it work?

If we've made all the right connections, after a few minutes we should see the display come on. (If there's a switch, make sure it's on!) Our lemon battery is producing a charge by having two different metals (aluminum and copper) in an acid liquid (the juice of the lemon). A chemical reaction takes place, which also produces an electrical charge. The electricity is conducted through the lemon juice, into the metal, and on into the circuit.

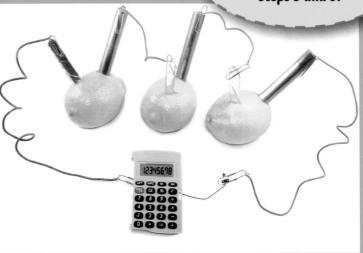

Step 6

Connect the "+" wire to the foil and the "−" wire to copper. In between, make sure copper connects to aluminum (foil). Ask an adult to help.

This Page Is Alarmed!

Now that we know how to make a circuit with a battery, lamp, and switch, it's time to put our knowledge to good use! We are going to make a simple alarm system. It's operated by an intruder stepping on a special switch called a pressure mat.

You will need

- 2 thin sheets of card roughly 10 x 8 inches (25 x 20 cm), bigger if you like
- 2 sheets of tin foil—the same area as the cardboard
- Thin sponge sheet (sold in craft stores)
- 2 paper clips
- 2 long pieces of wire with stripped ends
- The circuit from page 237
- Glue stick
- Small buzzer (from a hardware store)

Step 1

Stick foil to both sheets of card.

Step 2

Cut the sponge into strips about 1 inch (2.5 cm) wide.

Step 3

Stick the sponge strips on one foil-covered sheet with a glue stick.

244